Through Love's Difficult Times

We'll Grow Together

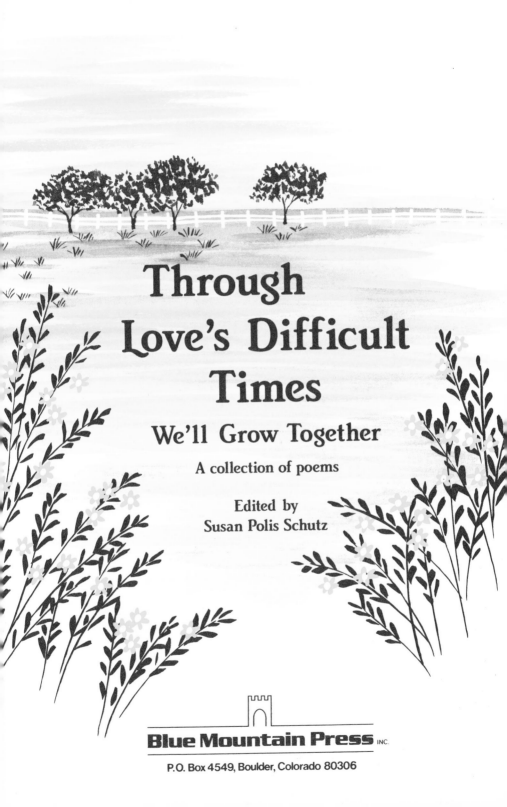

Through Love's Difficult Times

We'll Grow Together

A collection of poems

Edited by
Susan Polis Schutz

Blue Mountain Press INC.

P.O. Box 4549, Boulder, Colorado 80306

Library of Congress Number: 85-72419
ISBN: 0-88396-236-5

The following works have previously appeared in Blue Mountain Arts publications:

"In order to have a successful relationship," by Susan Polis Schutz. Copyright © Stephen Schutz and Susan Polis Schutz, 1980. "I don't always know," by Jamie Delere; and "I'm still learning about love," by Andrew Tawney. Copyright © Blue Mountain Arts, Inc., 1982. "Things aren't always perfect," by Susan Polis Schutz. Copyright © Stephen Schutz and Susan Polis Schutz, 1983. "I know things aren't always," by Jamie Delere; "I want 'more' for us" and "We've been through some hard times," by Lindsay Newman; "A special thought . . . ," "I sometimes feel," and "I Want Us to Be . . . ," by Laine Parsons; and "I know it's hard for us," by amanda pierce. Copyright © Blue Mountain Arts, Inc., 1983. "Don't be afraid to love," by Susan Polis Schutz. Copyright © Stephen Schutz and Susan Polis Schutz, 1984. "I'm taking a chance," by Karen Reibling. Copyright © Blue Mountain Arts, Inc., 1984. "Sometimes I don't like you . . . ," by Margo Walczak; "Life has been tough," by Donna Levine; "We've been through rough times," by Doug Konst; "I am so frightened," by Paula Lemley; and "Would You Tell Me?" and "I'm trying," by Collin McCarty. Copyright © Blue Mountain Arts, Inc., 1985. All rights reserved.

Thanks to the Blue Mountain Arts creative staff.

ACKNOWLEDGMENTS appear on page 62.

Manufactured in the United States of America
First printing: September, 1985

Blue Mountain Press INC.

P.O. Box 4549, Boulder, Colorado 80306

CONTENTS

I don't always know
how to tell you . . .
I'm not sure
how to let you know
when I'm worried
   or wondering . . .
About whether our
   relationship
   is okay, and whether
you're as happy
as you want to be.
I want you to know
that I don't always
have things figured out;
that I need your help sometimes
   and your reassurance . . .
and sometimes I need
just to have you hold me;
to let me know
that it's okay
and that we'll make it
   together through the hard times,
   appreciating all the good times,
hand in hand,
love
   in
      love.

— Jamie Delere

Give Us a Chance

I wish I could take back the things I said — take back the things I did. I know I can't; I can only hope to make up for the hurts I caused you.

Maybe you can never go back — but you can start again. If we both want it, we can make a new life together. I feel so fortunate to have our love . . . I do believe it can be better than it ever was.

It's not easy for either of us. But something worth having is never easy to come by. The more valuable the goal, the harder the fight — but the best part about this fight is we can both come out of it winners.

I don't expect change overnight.
I know it may be a long way to go,
but I'm willing to travel the distance
regardless of the outcome. I want us
to help each other, to grow together,
to achieve and feel the pride in each
other's accomplishments.
    Give us a chance; and give me a
chance to show you the love I have for you.

— K. J. LaFlam

Through love's difficult times . . .

Through love's difficult times,
I hope you'll agree that it's better
to appreciate the good times we had
than to regret or blame each other
    for the bad times,
and that the happiness we've shared
outweighs the pain we feel now.
Ours was an experience from which
    to learn and grow.

And regardless of how things work out,
you are still,
and always will be,
    an important person in my life.

                    — Paula Finn

Sometimes I don't like you . . .
     but I always love you.
There is a big difference
     between the two.
Loving lasts forever
     and grows deeper with
          the passage of time.
Liking is just a daily measurement
     of how one feels . . .
and so much depends upon
     what kind of mood I'm in
          or how my day has gone.

So even if I do become upset sometimes,
remember that it's only momentary,
     and that I'll be my
          normal self again soon.
And don't forget that even
     if I act like
          I don't always like you . . .

     I do always love you,
          and I always will.

                    — Margo Walczak

Life has been tough for us lately,
but it never was easy.
I hope these difficult times are
strengthening us and helping us
prepare for the changes we want to
bring about.
I hope we've learned from our mistakes
and past experiences.
Most of all,
I hope our feelings for each other
can survive these hard days,
and our love can grow deeper
with compassion and understanding.

Even stronger than these troubled times
is the fact that I love you more
than I ever thought possible,
and I want us to stay together.

— Donna Levine

It hasn't been easy for us lately;
it seems that there's always something
holding us apart.
It's not a question of who is to blame,
because we're both being ourselves,
and there's no fault in that.
I'm not sure what it is,
but I think that beneath it all,
we have something worthwhile.
If we can sort through all the confusion,
we can find the happiness we both want.
It isn't easy to do,
but I think our love is worth it.
I know you're worth it.

— Garry LaFollette

Things aren't always
perfect between us
but everything
worth anything
has flaws
in it
No one is perfect
therefore no
relationship can be perfect
Often by seeing
the dry brown petals
in a rose
you appreciate more
the vivid red petals
that are so beautiful
And I do appreciate
our very special relationship
which is so important to me
As we continue
to grow
as individuals
our relationship
will continue to grow
more beautiful
every day

— Susan Polis Schutz

I know things
aren't always sunshine and roses
    between us . . .
but don't worry;
everybody has their ups and downs,
    their happys and sads.
It's dealing with the
clouds and the thorns,
right along with the
    flowers and smiles
that serves to strengthen our
understanding of each other.

Let's just make sure
that we always build bridges
instead of walls,
with words instead of silence,
and with trust and care and love.

— Jamie Delere

We have to remember the love . . .

At times like these
it's easy to get discouraged
and to think of walking away.

But we have to remember
that the hurt and anger
come only because we really care.
And because we care,
we can draw on the strength of our
    affection
to see us through this difficult
period and beyond —
to the harmony and joy I know
    we can have.

It's easier to complain
than it is to work at making things
    better,
and lately we've fallen into a habit
    of concentrating too much
on the negatives in our relationship.

We need to dwell on our strengths
rather than our problems,
and focus on what we like in each other
rather than on what we'd like to change.
We have to forgive the bad times,
and look forward to the good.

We have to forget the hurt and anger . . .
    and we have to remember the love.

— Paula Finn

We've been through rough times,
and the hardest may be
yet to come.
But remember . . . the best things
in life
don't come easily.
Changes must sometimes
    be made,
and we must not be afraid
to make them.
For if we always remain
    the same,
we will fail to grow.
But if we can grow . . .
    together . . .
we will have a love
    that is known by
        so very few.

— Doug Konst

You are worth
every tear
that I will cry,
and worth all
the heartache
I will feel.

Loving you
isn't easy . . .
but it is worth
any chance that
needs to be taken . . .
just to have you
   in my life.

— Sheri Daugherty

I want "more" for us . . .

These days
when a relationship
isn't going very well,
it seems like most people
choose to take the easy way out.
Instead of working together
to find solutions to their
    problems,
they simply walk away from the
life they have made together.
They forget about the past
and leave behind all of the
    memories, the hopes,
        and the dreams.

I have a hard time thinking
about that happening to us.
The time that we've spent
sharing our lives together
has been very special for me,
and though we may not have
    very much,

what we do have is ours —
    yours and mine.
And where we are right now is
where together we decided that
we wanted to be —
    you and me.

I remember a time not so very
    long ago that
we thought our love was perfect,
and we looked forward to sharing
    that love forever
and to growing old
    . . . together.

Deep down inside, I have a feeling —
    the feeling that there is
    still love between you and me,
and I'm hoping you will agree
    that "we're" worth
        another try.

                — Lindsay Newman

I am so frightened
of losing what we've shared,
   what we have,
   what you've given me,
and most of all . . . of losing you.
I know we still talk,
   at times deeply;
somehow though, something's changed.
I sense an invisible, unspoken
   barrier between us . . .
      and it makes me wonder.
I don't want to feel this way.
I want to fight for us.
But I don't even know
      where to begin.

I only know . . . that I have
given so much of my soul to you,
    that should this ever end,
I could never be completely
    whole again.

I want to reach out to you
    and talk about it . . .
but it's frightening to think
    that for the first time
    . . . I'm not sure I can.

                        — Paula Lemley

In order to have
   a successful relationship
you need to put out of your mind
any lessons learned
   from previous relationships
because if you carry
   a sensitivity or fear with you
you won't be acting freely
and you won't let yourself
   be really known

In order to have
   a successful relationship
it is essential that both people
be completely open and honest

— Susan Polis Schutz

A special thought . . .

Sometimes it's not enough just to have you
in my life; there are times when I need
more of you than you give — more
attention, more understanding, maybe even
a little more of your time. Please understand.
I don't want to crowd you or ask too much.
I guess that I just want you to open up a
little bit more . . . share more of your thoughts
with me, your feelings and fears.

But most of all,
I want you to always remember
that you can trust me with your love;
and I want you to know that the more
of you you can give, the more of me
   you'll see smiling . . . with the wish
      to give nothing but
         good things back to you.

— Laine Parsons

In everyone's life
   there are problems to solve.
Even in the strongest relationship,
   there are differences to overcome.
It is easy to give up when confronted
   with difficulties;
to fool yourself into believing that
   perfection can be found
      somewhere else.
But true happiness and a lasting
   relationship are found
when you look inside yourself for
   solutions to the problems.
Instead of walking away when things
   get tough and blaming the other
      person,
look for compromise and forgiveness.

Caring is not a matter of convenience.
It is a commitment of one soul
   to another.
And if each gives generously of
   themselves, then both lives
      are enriched.
The problems will come and go,
   just like the changing seasons.
But unselfish love is constant
   and everlasting.

— Susan Staszewski

I'm taking a chance
    caring for you . . .
I know it,
    and it scares me,
    but it won't stop me . . .
because I see too much
        in you
to just let you slip by . . .
And I've learned
    that only through
    the risks
    and the reaching out
        for more
will there ever be
    a chance for all
        I've ever dreamed.

— Karen Reibling

I love you so much,
yet we are on such
    different wavelengths sometimes.
There are times when I wonder
how we will ever make it . . .
but so many other times when
I wonder how I could ever doubt
    that we will.
Despite any differences,
    we *will* always make it through,
    with . . .
        hard work and loyalty;
        trying to make things
        as good as possible;
    and through good times and bad,
        knowing that our hearts
        are bound to each other . . .
We are such good companions
    in friendship and in love.
            We'll make it.

— Jackie Brill Crothers

Trying to Understand . . .

It hurts when we don't understand
each other
When we struggle and fight to defend
what we believe to be right
Gambling on the strength of our love
frightened as children of losing
Yet persistent as lawyers at proving
our case
How sadly the hours go by
when our hearts are not at peace
I want you to know that I love you
and I know that loving is giving

Please help me . . .
because I really want to give.

— Jenny Sherman

Lately, it seems
we've been drifting
away from each other . . .
not terribly far,
but enough to be concerned.

I know things aren't
what they once were,
but that doesn't mean
they can't be again.

Every relationship
passes this point
at one time or another,
but the important thing
to remember is that
we can get through it.

It might not be easy —
worthwhile things
usually never are . . .

but if we really care
about one another,
and where we're headed
together,
maybe we can begin to
rediscover the things
that brought us together
in the beginning.

I care for you,
and I know you care for me.
Let's not stop here,
let's not give up
without a fight . . .
we're worth too much together.

— Keith Kennedy

I sometimes feel
a little jealous in my thoughts,
imagining that someone else
could please you more than me.
It's just my insecurity
acting up a bit, I guess . . .
because I know I'm not
the most beautiful,
the most enticing,
the most fun, or the
most imaginative person
in the world.
But I do know this —
that no matter
how much time goes by,
I can't imagine that
you'll ever find another
who will love you
with a beauty
and a passion
and a happiness
like that which I feel for you.

— Laine Parsons

We've been through some
hard times together —
    you and I.
Times that I look back on
and wonder how we ever
    made it through;
times when we both had
thoughts of giving up and
    going on alone,
but we always managed to
    see things through,
and I'm glad.

It seems like the hard times
never end for us,

but having someone like you
    to share them with
somehow makes it all seem
    a little easier.

So, I just wanted to take
    this time to say,
        "thanks" . . .
for your support,
    for your tolerance,
and most of all . . .
        for your love.

— Lindsay Newman

Sometimes
you are so distant
with me
that I can't help
but wonder if
I am still someone
special to you
Sometimes
you act as though
I am intruding
on your world
when all I really
want is to have you
share a part of mine
Sometimes
I feel as though
I have asked you
too many questions
when all I really
wanted was to
understand you
better.

— Yardley St. James

I Want Us to Be . . .

I know that
things are sort of difficult
right now for us . . .
but nobody ever said
it was going to be easy;
especially something
as important as the
blending of two lives into one.

I know that it's hard sometimes.
There are so many things
to be concerned about.
But at least we can do our part
by trying to realize what
the problems are, and then by
being flexible enough
to deal with them.

And if we really work at it,
if we really try . . .
we can become like a willow tree;
one that bends in the wind
instead of breaking,
and one that just grows stronger
and becomes more beautiful
with the passing of time.

— Laine Parsons

Don't be afraid
to love someone
totally and completely
Love is the most fulfilling
and beautiful feeling
    in the world
Don't be afraid that you will
get hurt
or that the other person
won't love you as much
as you love him
There is a risk in
everything you do
and the rewards
are never so great
as what love can bring
So let yourself get involved
completely and honestly
and enjoy the possibility
that what happens
might be the only real
source of happiness

— Susan Polis Schutz

I know that things haven't
been easy for us lately.
But a good relationship takes
effort and understanding
on both people's parts.

We need to set aside
old insecurities and stubbornness
and begin to listen with our
    hearts,
rather than with our pride.

We need to appreciate the other
person's side,
to hear the hurt behind the
    defenses,
to see the love behind the anger.

We must try to replace
accusation with forgiveness,
impatience with sensitivity,
and criticism with acceptance.

There's no reason to feel discouraged
or to think that things may never
be right again between us.
What we have built so far
is stronger than this temporary storm,
and looking beyond the clouds,
I can see the days of sunshine and
calm ahead.

I believe we can learn and grow
and develop our relationship
the way it was meant to be
if our motivation — and courage —
are strong enough.

I'm willing to work at it . . .
if you are.

— Paula Finn

I'm still learning about love,
so please be patient with me
when things go wrong, or
    when I hurt your feelings.
We have so much to look forward to,
and the time goes by so quickly . . .
that we should promise
never to allow a misunderstanding
to continue beyond a brief time.

We will deal with our concerns
as they come up . . . and our love
    will just get better, because . . .
we learn by doing,
and we grow by experiencing.

We've learned enough already to know
that love is made up of all things,
   the good with the difficult times,
   the quiet with the talkative times,
   the questions with the answers.

And even when I don't seem to know
   anything else . . .
I know that you're the answer
and the best thing in my life.

— Andrew Tawney

Would You Tell Me?

If you ever think you're
getting tired of our relationship,
              would you tell me?
Or if I ever do anything that upsets you,
will you share it instead of
    keeping it locked up inside?

I want you to come to me with your thoughts,
whether you think I want to hear them or not.
I need to know what's going on
    with your emotions — whether happy or sad.

And if you'll let me . . . I'll do
    the same for you . . . because I know
that communicating our fears
    right along with our fantasies,
and our difficulties
    right along with our dreams,
is one of the most important things
                        we can do.

The more we talk about things,
the better we will know that
instead of ever drifting apart,
we can make this relationship good and strong
    and give it the love and care to grow.

— Collin McCarty

I'm trying.
I really am.
But I just don't feel
   like I'm getting very far with you.

You must know how much I care.
And that I want us
   to make it through.
But I don't understand
why it has to be so hard.

I guess there are lots of things
I don't understand too well
   these days,
and too many things I don't know.

But I wish you would take the time
to help me with the most important
    question of all . . . so at least
    I'll know what to do from here . . .
since sometimes I don't know
whether to stay or to go . . .

Do you still love me?
Because if you do, please . . . tell me.
    I really need to know.

— Collin McCarty

I know it's hard for us
   sometimes . . .
Outside forces create pressures
   that affect our lives in
      unpredictable ways
Sometimes, we let our moods
   get the better of us;
our accomplishments fall short
   of our goals;
plans fall by the wayside;
and dreams seem too distant
   to hope for anymore . . .

But deep inside, I always
    carry our love,
and I know that we must never
stop working toward making
    things better . . .
After all . . .
we chose to be in this life
    together,
and with a little effort
    and understanding
and a lot of patience and love
that's exactly the way
    we're going to stay . . .
        happily together
            forever.

— amanda pierce

ACKNOWLEDGMENTS

We gratefully acknowledge the permission granted by the following authors to reprint their works.

K. J. LaFlam for "Give Us a Chance." Copyright © K. J. LaFlam, 1985. All rights reserved. Reprinted by permission.

Paula Finn for "I hope you'll agree," "We have to remember the love . . . ," and "I know that things haven't been easy." Copyright © Paula Finn, 1984. All rights reserved. Reprinted by permission.

Garry LaFollette for "It hasn't been easy for us." Copyright © Garry LaFollette, 1985. All rights reserved. Reprinted by permission.

Sheri Daugherty for "You are worth every tear." Copyright © Sheri Daugherty, 1984. All rights reserved. Reprinted by permission.

Susan Staszewski for "In everyone's life." Copyright © Susan Staszewski, 1982. All rights reserved. Reprinted by permission.

Jackie Brill Crothers for "I love you so much." Copyright © Jackie Brill Crothers, 1985. All rights reserved. Reprinted by permission.

Jenny Sherman for "Trying to Understand . . . ." Copyright © Jenny Sherman, 1985. All rights reserved. Reprinted by permission.

Keith Kennedy for "Lately, it seems we've been drifting." Copyright © Keith Kennedy, 1985. All rights reserved. Reprinted by permission.

Yardley St. James for "Sometimes you are so distant." Copyright © Yardley St. James, 1983. All rights reserved. Reprinted by permission.

A careful effort has been made to trace the ownership of poems used in this anthology in order to obtain permission to reprint copyrighted materials and to give proper credit to the copyright owners.

If any error or omission has occurred, it is completely inadvertent, and we would like to make corrections in future editions provided that written notification is made to the publisher: BLUE MOUNTAIN PRESS, INC., P.O. Box 4549, Boulder, Colorado 80306.